GALILEO G

A Life From Beginning to End

Copyright © 2017 by Hourly History

Table of Contents

Introduction
Living in the Italian Renaissance
Galileo's Early Life
Student Becomes Master
The Galilean Moons
Changing Worldviews
Opposition to the Church
Controversial Theories
The Trial of Galileo Galilei
The End of All Things
Galileo's Legacy
Conclusion

Introduction

In the world in which we live today, little thought is made of centuries past. There are the mandatory classes on world history, but we can no more know what life was about in those distant times than we can transport ourselves there. The past has passed, and we must get on with daily living.

However, there are those extraordinary people from history who bear discovering. There is something to be gleaned from who they were. One of these esteemed lives was Galileo Galilei. Born in the sixteenth century and living into the seventeenth century, Galileo was much more than a mere mathematician. It seems he touched on many interests in his life; from scientist to music-lover, there wasn't much he did not know of.

In addition to mathematics, Galileo in his lifetime, was a philosopher, engineer, physicist, and astronomer. He was a true polymath, or "Renaissance Man," a great thinker on many different levels. Galileo would go into the seventeenth century to play a significant role in the scientific revolution that had been brewing for some time.

It wouldn't be until later in his life that his discoveries and astronomical philosophies would come under attack. Galileo would stir up controversies that involved everyone; great scholars, esteemed friends and most of all, the Church, which would try to stifle all he knew to be true.

Galileo was a great man. Where that greatness came from is still being debated in the twenty-first century. He changed the world in ways others could not; not by all of the disciplines he surrounded himself with, but in the ways be brought controversies, arguments, and problems of his time to center-stage, where they came into conflict with the culture of the day. They needed to be addressed for they could no longer be denied or ignored.

Galileo's contributions in so many aspects of science are what keep his name still talked about today. Let us have a look at a noteworthy man and why he is still remembered five hundred years later.

Chapter One

Living in the Italian Renaissance

"To be great is to be misunderstood."

—Ralph Waldo Emerson

The Renaissance or New Birth in Europe was a time in history that took place between the fourteenth to the seventeenth centuries. It was the bridge on which history passed; going from medieval times into the modern age. It was into this time period that Galileo Galilei was born.

Mostly, the Renaissance was a cultural movement that profoundly affected all of European life. Prior to this, people were governed by the Catholic Church, and all life revolved around its holy days and doctrines.

In the mid-fourteenth century, around the year 1348, sickness began to visit Italy. It came with the sailors who had been in the East, and it quickly reached Genoa and Venice that year. No one knew what it was or how it spread; it would eventually be tied to the fleas on the rats who jumped onto the docks and settled in the cities.

In time, the Black Death, as it came to be known, devastated Europe. Every area was affected, and people died in droves. It is estimated that 30% to 60% of Europe's population died off. The plague didn't spare royalty, nor did it favor the clergy. Everyone was vulnerable.

Once the worst was passed, people were picking up their lives but realizing that there was a new philosophy in the air. Almost overnight it seemed, there were artists, writers, scientists, politicians, musicians, and philosophers who were expressing themselves in the humanist method. Where once works of art were created with no emotion attached to them, now it was the duty of the artist to display man and his works in all of their human glory.

What the Renaissance brought to the fourteenth century was a renewal of ideas from the ancient Greeks and Romans as well as attempts to study the secular and worldly views that were abounding. It was no longer a bad thing to want for yourself and your family; this, in turn, led to new ways of understanding your place in the world. It seemed as if Europe was about to explode with a cultural revolution never seen before.

This was the time of Leonardo da Vinci, Raphael, Michelangelo, Dante, Shakespeare, Sir Thomas More, Francis Bacon, and the Medicis. King Ferdinand and Queen Isabella, Henry VIII, Anne Boleyn, Queen Elizabeth I and kings and princes all across Europe and into Russia were commissioning artists for new churches, buildings, palaces, and museums.

From its humble beginnings in Italy where the idea of humanism flourished in Florence and Milan, the Renaissance ideas spread like wildfire throughout Europe. People were learning how to read and write, how to express their feelings, how to use their talents, all for the better.

It was into this very world that Galileo Galilei was born in 1564. This was the same year that William Shakespeare was born and the artist Michelangelo had died. It was a year to remember.

Chapter Two

Galileo's Early Life

"I am still learning."

—Michelangelo, age 87

Galileo Galilei was born in Pisa, Italy, which was in the duchy of Florence, on February 15, 1564. His parents were Vincenzo and Giulia, and they were married two years earlier. Galileo was the oldest of six children; three of his siblings survived infancy. Children dying at a very young age was very common right into the twentieth century.

Most written history has referred to Galileo as Galileo; his last name, Galilei, comes from an ancestor Galilei Bonaiuti, who was a doctor, university professor, and politician. The family changed their surname from Bonaiuti to Galilei in his honor.

The family was rich with culture and humanism. Galileo's father was a music theorist and composer, who lived to play the lute. One of Galileo's brothers was named Michelagnolo. He also became a famous composer and lutenist. It would have been from his father that Galileo learned to be skeptical of all authority and to appreciate the way in which music was composed. These revelations would lead him to a life of mathematics and experimentation.

When Galileo was eight years old, his family moved to Florence, Italy. This was the biggest and most culturally impressive city for a young boy to lay his eyes on. In 1574, Galileo began his formal education at the Camaldolese Monastery in Vallombrosa. The Camaldolese Order had split from the Benedictines in 1012. This combined the solitary life of the hermit with the strict life of a monk, and this appealed to the young Galileo.

Galileo had seriously considered joining the priesthood, but because his father insisted on a university education, he gave up the idea of becoming a monk. Instead, he enrolled in the University of Pisa in 1581 to study medicine. It wasn't long before he found himself interested in many other subjects as well. Mathematics and natural philosophy fascinated him—medicine not so much.

While he was at the University of Pisa, Galileo became familiar with the Aristotelian view of the world. Aristotelian logic is based on rationality developed by Aristotle. This philosophy relies on deductive reasoning and became popular in the Middle Ages and beyond. Aristotelian logic was the only one sanctioned by the Catholic Church.

Galileo at first supported this view as he was working towards getting his degree so he could teach at the university. Still, his real love was for mathematics, not being a physician. He continued to study mathematics with Filippo Fantoni, who headed up the department at the university. Even during summer vacations in Florence, Galileo continued to study his math.

In 1582 and 1583, a mathematician Ostilio Ricci taught a course on Euclid's Elements at the University of Pisa. Still resistant to his son learning about mathematics, Vincenzo desired Galileo to become a doctor. At this point, Galileo even invited Ricci to his home to try and convince Vincenzo that the young man should follow his interests in mathematics. Galileo's determination compelled Vincenzo to relent, just a little, and he allowed Galileo to study Euclid and Archimedes. By 1585, Galileo had left the university without getting his medical degree. Where Galileo was headed now was anybody's guess.

Chapter Three

Student Becomes Master

"You cannot teach a man anything, you can only help him find it within himself."

—Galileo Galilei

Galileo began teaching mathematics in 1585, first privately in Florence before moving onto Siena where he found a job. In the summer of the following year, he taught at Vallombrosa. It was here that Galileo invented a thermoscope, which was the forerunner of the thermometer. His first scientific book, *The Little Balance*, was published. This treatise had to do with the design of a hydrostatic balance he had invented. Hydrostatics is a branch of fluid mechanics and studies incompressible fluids at rest.

It was also at this time, in between teaching mathematics and finding a teaching position, that Galileo studied disegno, a term which encompassed all fine art. He was so inspired by all he saw in Florence, and by the Renaissance artists, that he obtained a position as instructor in the Accademia delle Arti del Disegno in Florence. Galileo taught perspective and chiaroscuro, which is an oil painting technique developed during this time. It uses deep contrasts between light and dark.

Paintings often look three-dimensional. While at the Accademia, Galileo made lifelong friends with artists. Even his love of mathematics was brought into his interests in the world of art.

By 1588, Galileo maintained a correspondence with his good friend Clavius, who was a professor of mathematics at the Jesuit Collegio Romano in Rome. Clavius liked the young student, and Galileo thought he would find favor in the search for a teaching position by knowing such an esteemed colleague. However, when an opening to teach mathematics came along at the University of Bologna, Galileo failed to gain that appointment.

Even after leaving Rome, Galileo stayed in contact with Clavius. He would discuss different theorems in his letters, such as the centers of the gravity of solids. Galileo wouldn't have received any course notes from his time at the Collegio Romano, so he copied out notes from classes there. Much of this material survives today.

Also, in 1588 Galileo received an attractive invitation from the Academy in Florence, to give a lecture about the dimensions and the location of Dante's Inferno. He wasn't established in any one place just yet, but that was about to change for the better.

The following year, an opening in the department of mathematics appeared at the University of Pisa and Galileo was appointed to fill the post. At first, this position seemed temporary, but quickly good things were being said about Galileo. His friend Clavius was giving him high praise, and he had also acquired an excellent reputation from the lectures he had given the previous year at the Florence Academy.

Galileo was to stay at the University of Pisa for three years. During this time he wrote a series of essays entitled *De Motu*. These dealt with the theory of motion and were never published. Galileo wasn't happy with how these pieces had turned out, and it was he who decided not release them. There were ideas in *De Motu* which would prove to be incorrect, but one of his better ideas was that theories could be tested through experimentation. One of the tests Galileo conducted was the idea that you could test theories about falling bodies using an inclined plane to slow the rate of descent.

In 1591, Galileo's father Vincenzo died. Being the eldest son, Galileo would be responsible for providing for his two younger sisters and his brother Michelagnolo. He would now be accountable for paying dowries for his sisters and for his younger brother's care. Being a professor in Pisa was just not getting the job done, so Galileo started looking elsewhere for a better-paying university position.

With a strong recommendation from a mathematician friend, Guidobaldo del Monte, Galileo was appointed a professor of mathematics at the University of Padua, which was the university at the Republic of Venice. By 1592, his salary was three times the rate he received at Pisa. Galileo started giving lectures in December and remained at Padua for the next 18 years.

This period in Galileo's life would be, according to him, the happiest time of his life. At the University of

Padua, he taught most on Euclid's geometry and geocentric astronomy to medical students. It would seem rather odd today to have to know something about astronomy to be a physician, but in the sixteenth century, understanding astronomy came in handy because it helped give a foundational base for astrology which was essential to making medical diagnoses in those centuries.

While teaching mathematics in Padua, Galileo was to make some crucial discoveries. He came across new findings in pure fundamental science, which included astronomy and kinematics of motion, as well as practical applied science—the design of newer telescopes—and he kept up his studies on astrology.

His love of mathematics would lead him to a love of the heavens as the years went by. Eventually, Galileo would bring new light to old controversies, ones which had been around since ancient times. But for now, he was content to live and love his life in Padua.

Chapter Four

The Galilean Moons

"Science would not be what it is if there had not been a Galileo, Newton, or a Lavoisier . . . the world as we know it is the product of its geniuses."

—Norman Robert Campbell

During his time in Padua, Galileo eventually fell in love with one Marina Gamba. He was, just like most people of his day, a pious Roman Catholic, but with Marina, Galileo fathered three children out of wedlock. They were never married.

A daughter, Virginia, was born in 1600 followed by a second daughter, Livia, the following year. A son, Vincenzo, named after Galileo's father, was born in 1606. Because the girls were illegitimate, they were considered unworthy to marry. Both daughters would end up in the convent where they remained until their deaths. Vincenzo, on the other hand, would be legitimized in later life as Galileo's legal heir.

When writing *De Motu*, his series of essays, Galileo had erred in his theory of motion. He believed that the force acting on a body was the relative difference between the specific gravity and also that of the substance through which it moved. In this belief, he was mistaken. By the time he wrote to a mathematician friend, Paolo Sarpi, in 1604, Galileo had realized his mistake. Two years previously, Galileo had returned to his study of the theory of motion. By this time, he had worked out the correct law of falling bodies through studying inclined planes and the pendulum.

Galileo figured out that a projectile followed a parabolic path. Projectile motion is a form of movement where an object moves in a bilaterally symmetrical way. The course that the object follows is called its trajectory. One force only is applied, and the only interference would be from gravity. These discoveries would not be published for 35 years.

By May 1609, Galileo was developing a new series of telescopes. He was able to do this because of his mathematical skills and his love of craftsmanship. These designs brought a new optical performance to astronomy. They were much improved on the Dutch instruments. To enhance the magnification of the lenses, Galileo learned how to grind and polish his own lenses, and come August; his telescope was six to nine times more magnification than previously.

Galileo realized almost immediately how his refined creations could help sailors at sea. His friend arranged for a demonstration in front of the Venetia Senate. They were truly impressed with this innovation, and in return for a major increase in salary, Galileo gave away all his rights to the manufacture of his telescopes to the Venetian Senate. Later in life, he would repeat the notion that the telescope was never his invention anyway, so rights to it were, in fact, meaningless.

However, others would disagree. With a Galilean telescope, anyone looking through it could see much magnified, upright images on land. It was one of a kind at the time because it also made it possible to view the skies above. By the end of 1609, Galileo realized that telescopes were meant for more important things than scanning the earthly horizons. He began turning his gaze to the night sky. He surely could not have anticipated what remarkable discoveries were waiting to be found there.

The mathematician Galileo was slowly morphing into a scientist. In March 1610, he published a small treatise called *Sidereus Nuncius* (The Starry Messenger). In this famous work, Galileo talked about his observations of the moon and more importantly, his discovery and studies of the four moons orbiting the planet Jupiter. According to Galileo, the surface of the moon was not smooth, and there were many craters to be found there, as well as mountains.

Suddenly the Aristotelian world-view which everyone believed in from ancient times was being challenged. This view held that everything above the Earth was perfect and incorruptible.

Galileo was able to see the line separating lunar day from night, also called the terminator, and he deduced that the darker regions of the moon are flat and low-lying areas, while the brighter regions are rougher and mountainous. Amazingly, he correctly judged the mountains to be about four miles high.

With his telescope, Galileo was able to see at least ten times more stars than one could see without using a telescope. He published star charts of the belt of Orion and of the Pleiades, which is a tiny star cluster visible to the naked eye. Finally, Galileo reported that he had discovered four objects that seen through the telescope appeared to form a straight line of stars near Jupiter.

In making observations of these four objects from January through March 1610, Galileo concluded that the bodies changed their positions relative to Jupiter, yet always stayed in a straight line. This made Galileo believe these objects were orbiting the giant planet. Initially, he called the four moons the Medician Stars, naming them for four royal Medici brothers. This helped him greatly in attaining prestigious positions at the University of Pisa, but the name never stuck. The moons of Jupiter are always referred to as the Galilean moons.

When Galileo published *The Starry Messenger*, many individuals were skeptical. Reactions ranged from great praise to disbelief to hostility. Some people believed that the lens was defective and that what Galileo was seeing was just an illusion. As for the moon being rough and irregular, this flew in the face of the accepted conception about the heavens at the time. God had made a perfect universe and who was Galileo to say otherwise?

By autumn, however, several other astronomers were able to observe the moons and confirm Galileo's discoveries. Io, Europa, Ganymede, and Callisto are the names that were finally given to the four moons of Jupiter.

Still, scientists and the general public felt that Galileo's depiction of the moon as irregular directly contradicted what the ancient astronomer Ptolemy had observed. Aristotle had described the cosmos as perfect and unchanging heavenly bodies. Now, conflict ensued.

Chapter Five

Changing Worldviews

"In questions of science, the authority of a thousand is not worth the humble reasoning of a single individual."

—Galileo Galilei

Once Galileo's little book *The Starry Messenger* was published, he resigned his post at Padua and returned to Pisa to become Chief Mathematician at the university. In 1611, he visited Rome and was treated like a celebrity. The Collegio Romano gave lavish dinners in his honor, and Galileo was also made a member of the Accademia dei Lincei, a distinction which Galileo prized for the rest of his life. Galileo was particularly proud of the tribute bestowed by the Accademia dei Lincei, so much so that from that point forward he always signed his name "Galileo Galilei Linceo." He had become the sixth member to join the esteemed Accademia.

From the time he was in Rome, and then upon his return to Florence, Galileo was fascinated with his four moons of Jupiter. He was able to roughly establish the orbital periods for the four moons after making observations through his telescope, but he was finding that more precise calculations were harder to come by. It was a struggle to identify which moon was which. He set out to observe the moons over an extended time frame, and by 1612, Galileo was able to give accurate periods of each moon of Jupiter.

At first, his calculations seemed off. Galileo couldn't explain why. Then he realized he had not been taking into account the motion of the Earth revolving around the sun. All in all, Galileo's observations of the moons of Jupiter were causing quite a commotion. After all, these discoveries did not hold with the principles of Aristotelian cosmology, which held that all heavenly bodies should circle the Earth. Many leading astronomers and philosophers of the day refused to believe that a man like Galileo could have uncovered such a momentous discovery.

Galileo had persevered, and by the end of 1611, his observations were so accurate that what he was recording had to be paid attention to. One of Galileo's contemporaries was Johannes Kepler, a German scientist and astronomer. Kepler had always believed that obtaining accurate estimates for the four moons of Jupiter was absolutely impossible.

In the summer of 1610, Galileo then turned his telescope on the planet Saturn. At first, it looked like three bodies because Galileo's telescope wasn't strong enough to show Saturn's rings; rather they appeared to him to be separate globes circling around the planet itself. Galileo continued to observe Saturn, and whenever the ring system was edge on, it disappeared altogether. Galileo was puzzled.

Also through his telescope, Galileo observed that the planet Venus showed phases like those of the moon. He concluded this planet must orbit the Sun and not the Earth. At the time, most if not all astronomers believed in the system put forth by a Danish astronomer named Tycho Brahe. Brahe surmised that everything but the Earth and the Moon went round the Sun, which in turn orbits the Earth. The other way of looking at the heavens was the Copernican system, where all bodies orbit the Sun.

Nicolaus Copernicus had been born a generation before Galileo, and he supported the heliocentric system in astronomy. His work, *On the Revolutions of the Celestial Spheres*, was published in 1543, the year of his death. It was met with only mild controversy. Nothing or no one had yet backed this theory, and it was just another way of observing what could be in the heavens, but would most likely be proven wrong eventually.

So, at the time Galileo was making his observations one could believe in the heliocentric system or the Tychonic system. Because the instruments of the day were not powerful enough to decide between the two, there was no way of making a clear distinction. Despite this, Galileo knew that all his discoveries were evidence of a Copernican system, even if right at that moment, he didn't have sufficient proof to challenge the conventional opinion.

This was where Galileo's theory of falling bodies came into play. He had earlier conducted experiments at the Tower of Pisa and in so doing, Galileo had been able to refute the old Aristotelian notion that heavier objects fall faster than lighter ones. When he performed experiments at the tower, he dropped two spheres of different weight and watched as they hit the ground at the exact same time.

At the time, most people believed the Earth was stationary; that it did not move. Galileo knew from his falling bodies theory that this was not so. Opponents of a moving Earth argued that if the Earth rotated and a body was dropped from a high place, such as a tower, it should fall behind where it was dropped as the Earth turned as it fell. This was not observed in practice, so most people believed the Earth did not move at all.

However, Galileo knew otherwise. And as his astronomical observations continued, there would be more revelations about the world and the heavens.

Chapter Six

Opposition to the Church

"Somewhere, something incredible is waiting to be known."

—Carl Sagan

Observations on the skies above have been going on since ancient times. Ptolemy, a Greek scientist, living in Alexandria Egypt in the second century C.E. had noticed and concluded that there was a geocentric theory of the heavens. He put forth that the Sun and all the heavenly bodies rotated around the Earth.

Copernicus had said that the Sun was the center of everything and he developed the heliocentric system. Once Galileo started observing the phases of the planet Venus, he concluded that the Ptolemaic system—or the Tychonic system which was based on the Ptolemaic— would no longer do. By the early seventeenth century, most astronomers had converted to the Copernican system for observing the heavens. This was due in part to Galileo's observations of all of the phases of Venus, which made the change-over from full geocentrism to full heliocentrism.

In 1612, Galileo made a new exciting discovery in the form of the planet Neptune. At first, he saw it as one of many unremarkable dim stars. Subsequently, he was able to note its motion relative to the stars and lost sight of it.

Galileo made other observations which included viewing sunspots. He made naked-eye and telescopic observations of sunspots. He published his findings in *Discourse on Floating Bodies* which he released in 1612. The following year *Letters on the Sunspots* came out.

The Milky Way was also an object of Galileo's fascination. Scientists often didn't know what to make of this and thought it was what was referred to as nebulous or consisting of clouds of dust, hydrogen, helium and other gases in outer space. Galileo, however, realized the Milky Way was a multitude of stars packed together so tightly that they appeared like clouds when observing them on the Earth.

He was able to tell the difference between stars and planets. When viewing them through the telescope, Galileo described stars as mere blazes of light and planets which the telescope revealed to be discs. He was able to come up with a way of measuring the apparent size of stars without a telescope.

Galileo was very much in favor of Copernicanism, where the Sun was the center of all heavenly bodies. He knew this was a controversial thing among the public and went out of his way to avoid arguments about the issue. Eventually, as with all things, he was drawn into the discussion by the chair of mathematics in Pisa in 1613. His name was Castelli, and he had once been a student of Galileo's and was also in favor of Copernicanism.

In December, a meeting took place at the Medici palace in Florence. In attendance was the Grand Duke Cosimo II and his mother the Grand Duchess Christina of Lorraine. Castelli was asked to explain his position about Copernicanism and how it conflicted with Holy Scripture. He defended the heliocentric or Copernican position passionately. Afterward, he wrote to Galileo telling him how he had successfully defended this position. However, Galileo was not equally convinced. He wrote a letter to Castelli, and in it, he argued that the Bible should be interpreted in light of what science was revealing to the world.

Several people were opponents of Galileo, and they sent a copy of his letter to the Inquisition in Rome. But, there was little there that they could object to, so nothing came of it. Keep in mind that the Church ran all things in the early 1600s in Italy. The Reformation was already underway, but its influence was not as greatly felt in Italy as it was in other countries, such as England and northern Europe. So it was no surprise that the Catholic Church's most prominent figure at the time was Cardinal Robert Bellarmine. Anytime there was a need for an interpretation of Holy Scripture it was to Cardinal Bellarmine that the Church would turn.

At this time, around 1615, Bellarmine saw little reason for the Church to be concerned with the Copernican theory. What some were worried about was whether or not Copernicus had put forth his mathematical theory which enabled the calculations of all of the heavenly bodies to be viewed in a simpler way—or whether he was now introducing a new physical reality.

So, at the time, neither Copernicus nor Galileo seemed to be threatening the structure of the Church at all. Nothing they were putting forward was anything more than pure theory. Then, in 1616 Galileo wrote a letter to the Grand Duchess, and in it, he vehemently attacked the followers of Aristotle.

The message struck a nerve. Galileo said that the Copernican system was much more than a theory; it was an actual and physical reality. He stated:

"I hold that the Sun is located at the center of the revolutions of the heavenly orbs and does not change place, and that the Earth rotates on itself and moves around it. Moreover, . . . I confirm this view not only by refuting Ptolemy's and Aristotle's arguments, but also by producing many for the other side, especially some pertaining to physical effects whose causes perhaps cannot be determined in any other way, and other astronomical discoveries; these discoveries clearly confute the Ptolemaic system, and they agree admirably with this other position and confirm it."

The Pope, Paul V, ordered Bellarmine to have the Sacred Congregation make a decision regarding the Copernican theory. By this time, Galileo's writings had been submitted to the Inquisition stating that he and his followers were attempting to reinterpret the Bible. It was a violation set down by the Council of Trent and looked a lot like Protestantism, which had blossomed in the early 1500s.

On February 24, 1616, the cardinals of the Inquisition got together. They began gathering evidence from theological experts. Subsequently, they condemned the teachings of Copernicus, and Cardinal Bellarmine notified Galileo of their findings. Galileo himself had not been invited to this trial.

An Inquisitorial commission declared heliocentrism to be "foolish and absurd in philosophy, and formally heretical since it explicitly contradicts in many places the sense of Holy Scripture." Hence, Galileo was ordered not to put forth Copernican theories anymore. He was no longer to utter any ideas that heliocentrism was true. A decree was created banning the works of Copernicus and other heliocentric works until they could be corrected.

As luck would have it, Galileo need not have worried. One of his admirers, Maffeo Barberini, was elected as Pope Urban VIII. Galileo was getting ready to publish his new book, *The Assayer*, and dedicated the book to the pope.

Pope Urban invited Galileo to six different papal audiences and led Galileo to believe that the suppression of Copernican theories would not result in any noticeable changes. Galileo went ahead published his views, thinking no repercussion would come of his further studies and findings.

Up until this point in history, the Christian worldview held to the Aristotelian geocentric view that the Earth was at the center of the universe, or the system put forth by Tycho Brahe, that was a blend of geocentrism and heliocentrism. Once Copernicus died, and before Galileo, heliocentrism was never viewed as much of an issue.

Religious opposition to heliocentrism seemed to be backed by Biblical references. There are areas in the Old Testament which say things such as "the world is firmly established, it cannot be moved." And Ecclesiastes 1:5 states that "the sun rises and sets and returns to its place." So, where were these astronomers coming up with their opposing theories?

Chapter Seven

Controversial Theories

*"I think great artists and great engineers are similar, in
that they both have a desire to express themselves."*

—Steve Jobs

Galileo put forth many correct theories about the heavens.
But, he wasn't always right. One of those times was in
1618 when three comets came into sight, and he became
involved in their appearance. He believed that the comets
were close to the Earth and caused by optical refraction or
a change in light waves due to a change in their
transmission.

Trouble seemed to loom on the horizon for Galileo.
The more he argued, the more he made himself an enemy
of the Jesuits. Then, in 1619, Galileo found himself
embroiled in an argument with Father Orazio Grassi who
was a professor of mathematics at the Jesuit Collegio
Romano. At first, it was nothing more than a
disagreement about the nature of comets, but in a few
years had escalated to something more.

Earlier that year, Father Grassi had also published a
pamphlet anonymously titled *An Astronomical
Disputation on the Three Comets of the Year 1618*. The
previous year, in November, to be exact, a comet had

appeared in the night sky. Grassi had concluded that this comet was a fiery body which moved along at a great distance from the Earth. Because it moved in the sky more slowly than the moon, Grassi said it must be farther away than the Moon.

Grassi's conclusions were criticized by one of Galileo's followers, a lawyer from Florence, one Mario Guiducci. Galileo and Guiducci didn't offer any theory of their own regarding comets, although they did throw out some ideas, which are now known to be mistaken.

Galileo and Guiducci had published a work called *Discourse on the Comets*, where their theories were made known. In addition to this, the authors also made uncomplimentary remarks about the professors at the Collegio Romano. The Jesuits were offended, to say the least, and Grassi followed up with a tract of his own entitled *The Astronomical and Philosophical Balance*.

By this time, Galileo had also published *The Assayer*, and in it, he takes apart Grassi's arguments one by one. Many people loved this tract and the pope, Urban VIII, was a particular fan. Now, Galileo had permanently alienated many of the Jesuits who had formally been on his side. He always believed that it was the Jesuits who brought about the condemnation he suffered in later years.

From 1618 and on into the next decade, Galileo tried to stay far away from further controversies. He decided to write a book on the subject of heliocentrism anyway because the Pope was a good friend of his, and someone who he believed would be on his side.

As time went on, Galileo's health was declining, and he was having frequent bouts of severe illness. By 1624, Galileo started writing his book, his famous *Dialogue Concerning the Two Chief World Systems*. In 1630, when his work was finally completed, Galileo even requested permission from Rome to publish the book, but it was not an easy task.

Eventually, he did receive permission from Florence, not Rome. It was inevitable that now things would come to a head where once again, Church and State clashed. Or in this case, it was more like Church and Astronomer.

Chapter Eight

The Trial of Galileo Galilei

"I do not feel obliged to believe that the same God who has endowed us with sense, reason, and intellect has intended us to forgo their use."

—Galileo Galilei

There are trials, and then there are trials. Back in the 1930s, there was the famous Lindbergh trial, where Bruno Richard Hauptmann was put on trial for the kidnapping and murder of the son of Charles Lindbergh. In the 1990s the sensational O.J. Simpson trial had the world transfixed. Similarly, in the 1630s it was Galileo who was facing the wrath of the powers that be in Rome.

All this, because Galileo was trying to stay on the side of what he knew to be correct thinking about the cosmos. For centuries, dating back to the Greek and Roman eras, most theories about the heavens stayed very much in sync with the Catholic Church, which was the dominating power of the age.

The trial of Galileo was a critical moment in Western culture because it brought to a point the stormy relationship that had always existed between science and religion. Most people imagine Galileo standing before a panel of sour-looking judges, then made to kneel he is forced to say all of the false things about theories which he knew were outdated and of no significance any longer. But, when he stands up he stamps his foot on the ground and stubbornly declares, "Still it moves."

Actually, the trial was nothing like that at all. But, from the preceding years, especially the year 1616 when Rome had formally banished all thought of the heliocentric idea of what comprised the solar system, they had laid down their ruling in hard, cold stone. Now, here was Galileo again.

Galileo's book, *Dialogue*, was formally published in 1632 with papal permission and officially authorized by the Inquisition. At this point in his life, it was apparent that Galileo had done many things over the years; things which were astonishing, to say the least. He was brilliant in mathematics and physics, published numerous papers and tracts on the subjects, and his experiments in astronomy were second to none among those living at the time.

Galileo had been a genius thinker from his teen years. From the age of 19, when he discovered the isochronism of the pendulum, to when at age 22, he had invented the hydrostatic balance. By the time he was a mere 25-year-old, he was giving his first lectures at the University of Pisa and was known as a brilliant speaker. All of Europe had quickly come to know who Galileo Galilei was.

Earlier, Pope Urban VIII had requested that Galileo give arguments both for and against heliocentrism, but he didn't want Galileo to support heliocentrism. He also requested that his own views on the matter also be included in the book. Galileo only followed the second demand.

In the book *Dialogue*, the form of the book is between people, Salviati, who argues for the Copernican system and Simplicio, who is a follower of Aristotle. At the end of the book, Galileo has Salviati articulating that the Earth moves, which was based on Galileo's theory of the tides. Johannes Kepler had put out the correct theory showing that Galileo's theory of the tides was false. Aside from this error, there were noteworthy truths put forth in *Dialogue*.

When reading *Dialogue*, there were those who believed Galileo's Simplicio was an attack on Aristotelian geocentrism and for favoring heliocentrism. After all, the word "simplicio" in Italian, denotes "simpleton." To make matters worse, Galileo put the words of Pope Urban into the mouth of Simplicio.

Most historians believe Galileo did not act in a vengeful way towards the pope. In fact, he was caught rather by surprise when so much negative reaction began reaching him concerning his *Dialogue*. The Pope was outraged and summoned Galileo to Rome to stand trial.

Unfortunately for Galileo, it didn't matter if the pope was a good friend or not, he had finally turned one of his biggest supporters against him. The Inquisition banned the sale of his book and ordered Galileo to Rome in September 1632. Because of illness, Galileo wasn't able to make the trip until February the following year.

So, Galileo was now being tried for advocating for a new world-view; heliocentrism. He was almost 70 years old and in poor health, and he was on trial for his life. His proceedings would be conducted by the Congregation of the Holy Office, popularly known as the Roman Inquisition. Ten cardinals would preside, all of whom had been appointed by the pope. It was their job to safeguard Catholic dogma and to prevent any and all attacks against it.

In an almost unprecedented move, Galileo was not imprisoned during his trial. Rather he was allowed to live at the Villa Medici, the Tuscan ambassador's residence in Rome. The trial was completed in three sessions; April 12, April 30 and May 10.

When the trial began, Galileo was asked why he thought he was summoned to Rome for trial and the standard answer would have been to say "no." After all, to go on at length at the accusations against him would immediately have put him in a bad light, making it obligatory for him to begin defending himself. But, Galileo boldly replied he thought he was there because of his book *Dialogue*.

Right away, the questions turned to the year 1616 and Galileo's affairs in Rome. He said he came to Rome on his own to learn what he was allowed to say concerning Copernicanism, also known as the heliocentric theory. He said he had been informed by Cardinal Bellarmine, that the heliocentric theory could only be spoken of lightly and no truth could be taken from it, as it went against Church doctrine.

The questioning escalated and became more heated, and Galileo produced a letter he had received from

Cardinal Bellarmine, dated three months after he had met with him in February 1616. It read:

"We, Robert Cardinal Bellarmine, hearing that it has been calumniously rumored that Galileo Galilei had abjured in our hands and also has been given a salutory penance, and being requested to state the truth with regard to this, declare that this man Galileo has not abjured, either in our hands or in the hands of any other person here in Rome, or anywhere else as far as we know, any opinion or doctrine which he has held; nor has any salutory or any other kind of penance been given to him. Only the declaration made by the Holy Father and published by the Sacred Congregation of the Index has been revealed to him, which states that the doctrine of Copernicus, that the earth moves around the sun and that the sun is stationary in the center of the universe and does not move east to west, is contrary to Holy Scripture and therefore cannot be defended or held. In witness whereof we have written and signed this letter with our hand on this twenty-sixth day of May 1616."

The court had no idea Galileo was going to produce such a letter. Bellarmine's order to Galileo was clear enough; it was simply "not to hold or defend Copernicanism." There was a memo from the Holy Office which stated that the Commissary General, not Bellarmine, had issued an injunction against Galileo. In it was said that Galileo could not "hold, teach or defend it in any way, either verbally or in writing." The essence of what Bellarmine had said to Galileo would have denied Galileo permission to deal with Copernicanism even in a hypothetical way. This was supposed to be the very key piece of evidence introduced at the trial, and now two pieces of evidence contradicted each other.

Galileo had no idea what questions would be asked him, but he had kept his precious letter from Cardinal Bellarmine, almost as an insurance policy, should anyone question his actions. The court asked Galileo if there were witnesses to the injunction or had someone that Galileo had forgotten about, still said he would not be allowed to speak or write about Copernicanism. Galileo stated that he did not remember anyone else intervening.

The Court then turned to the published book *Dialogue*. Did the book have an imprimatur? This is the seal given by the Holy See, still in practice today, that the Church is certifying there is nothing contrary to Catholic faith and teaching. Galileo went on to state he was given not just one imprimatur, but two. This was indeed a dilemma. How could the Church bring to trial someone who had written a book which the Church itself had approved of?

The accusation brought against Galileo was that he had breached the conditions set down by the Inquisition in 1616. All throughout his trial, Galileo vigorously maintained that he had not gone public with any of his opinions, which the Church was condemning him for. At first, he denied even defending them.

As his trial went on, Galileo was persuaded to admit that any reader of his book, *Dialogue*, would have come away with the impression that it was a defense of Copernicanism. Galileo denied that he had held

Copernican ideas after 1616 and he vehemently denied that he had intended to defend them in his book.

Towards the end of his trial in July 1633, Galileo was interrogated harshly and threatened with torture if he did not tell the truth. Despite having this thrown in his face, he maintained his denial. The case against Galileo was weak, and there were some who wanted a speedy end to it. At the same time, Galileo was falling ill again. He was afflicted with pains, some so bad that he cried out in the night. He was given medicine, and it was deemed not possible to move out of where he was staying. Everyone knew that a swift conclusion would be the best thing.

Pressure continued to build on those who had brought charges against Galileo. The Church denied Copernicanism or heliocentrism. This was their position since 1616, and they had not changed their stance. The prosecutor was authorized to strike a plea bargain with Galileo. He would plead guilty to some minor offense in writing his book, for a lighter sentence.

Finally, the sentence was passed down in three parts. Galileo had asked the Court to consider his ill health, the fact that he was close to 70 years old and that many had already slandered him over and over, and this was felt by him to be a just punishment.

The first part found Galileo "vehemently suspect of heresy," because he had held the opinions that the Sun is at the center of the universe and sits there motionless. Because Holy Scripture held the Aristotelian geocentric view, Galileo had therefore gone against the Church. He was required to "abjure, curse, and detest" these opinions.

Secondly, the Inquisition would decide where he would be imprisoned. This confinement would be for the rest of Galileo's life. The day after judgment was rendered, they commuted his sentence to house arrest.

Last, Galileo's disturbing book which had prompted the charges was banned. Additionally, all works published by Galileo were prohibited, as well as anything he might write in the future. Galileo was relieved with the outcome, for he wasn't certain of what the conclusions would be.

At first, Galileo stayed with the archbishop of Siena. Then he was allowed to return to his villa at Arcetri near Florence in 1634. He would remain there under house arrest for the rest of his life.

In the seventeenth century, court proceedings were not carried out as they are today in a modern courtroom. There were no legal guarantees of due process, such as being represented by competent counsel. Galileo defended himself. These were church courts which handled or mishandled evidence as it was presented to them, and there is no way to ascertain how just or unjust the findings were.

As part of his punishment, Galileo was ordered to pray the seven penitential psalms, once a week, for the next three years. These psalms are 6, 32, 38, 51, 102, 130, and 143. His eldest daughter, now known as Sister Maria Celeste, secured ecclesiastical permission to take the reading of these psalms unto herself. The request was granted. Unfortunately, it was also in 1634 that this beloved daughter, only 33 years old, died. She had been the greatest support to her father all through his troubles and tribulations, and he took her death very hard. He did not resume work again for many months.

Chapter Nine

The End of All Things

"Copernicus, Galileo and Kepler did not solve an old problem, they asked a new question, and in doing so they changed the whole basis on which the old questions had been framed."

—Ken Robinson

When Galileo did decide to write again, he started on the project that would come to be known as *Discourses and Mathematical Demonstrations Concerning the Two New Sciences* . This book would prove to be one of his finest works, and it was smuggled out of Italy and taken to Holland where it was published.

In *Discourses*, Galileo summed up much of his work over the last 40 years, on two new sciences, kinematics and strength of materials. He also touched on some of the theories he left unpublished in *De Motu* in 1590 and talked about such things as impetus, moments and centers of gravity. One of the people who highly praised this book was Albert Einstein. This is the reason many people often refer to Galileo as the "father of modern physics."

By 1638, Galileo was suffering from insomnia and a painful hernia. He was allowed to travel to Florence to seek medical advice. Galileo continued to receive visitors until the year of his death. By this time he was suffering from fevers and heart palpitations and at age 77, Galileo died on January 8, 1642.

A Grand Duke of Tuscany wanted Galileo buried in the Basilica of Santa Croce, next to his father, but Pope Urban reminded him that Galileo had been condemned by the Catholic Church for heresy. Instead, Galileo was buried in a small room next to the novices' chapel at the end of a hallway. In 1737, he was reburied in the main body of the basilica, when a monument had been erected there in his honor. During the move, three fingers and a tooth were removed. If you visit the Museo Galileo in Florence, Galileo's middle finger from his right hand is on display.

The Inquisition's ban on reprinting Galileo's works was finally lifted in 1718, when editions of his books, with the exception of *Dialogue*, were published in Florence. By the mid-1700s, Pope Benedict XIV allowed all of Galileo's works to be issued, including his *Dialogue*, making sure it was mildly censored. Then in 1758, the general prohibition against works advocating heliocentrism was removed from the index of prohibited books. However, there was still a specific ban on Copernicus' *De Revolutionibus* and Galileo's *Dialogue*.

It was in 1835 that these works, too, were dropped from the index. In 1939, Pope Pius XII described Galileo as being among the "the most audacious heroes of research . . . not afraid of the stumbling blocks and the risks on the way, nor fearful of the funereal monuments." The pope, during this day of age, was not closing any doors to science prematurely. He regretted what had happened to Galileo.

On February 15, 1990, Cardinal Ratzinger, who would go on to be elected Pope Benedict XVI, gave a speech at the Sapienza University of Rome. He cited current views about the Galileo affair. Ratzinger called to mind the philosopher Paul Feyerabend, who had said, "The Church at the time of Galileo kept much more closely to reason than did Galileo himself, and she took into consideration the ethical and social consequences of Galileo's teaching too. Her verdict against Galileo was rational and just and the revision of this verdict can be justified only on the grounds of what is politically opportune."

Ratzinger didn't make it clear where he stood in regard to Feyerabend's assessment of Galileo. He did feel that an impulsive apology would be foolish at the time.

On October 31, 1992, Pope John Paul II expressed regret for how the Galileo affair was conducted. The pope issued a declaration which acknowledged the errors committed by the Catholic Church tribunal that had judged the scientific positions held by Galileo, as the result of a study conducted by the Pontifical Council for Culture. Then, in March 2008, the head of the Pontifical Academy of Sciences announced that a statue of Galileo himself would be erected inside the Vatican's walls. However, in January 2009, the Academy announced it wouldn't be putting up the Galileo statue after all.

Chapter Ten

Galileo's Legacy

"I've loved the stars too fondly to be fearful of the night."

—Galileo Galilei

Galileo was, believe it or not, one of the founders of modern science. What has been rendered possible in the twenty-first century was imagined and invented in centuries past, in worlds such as the Renaissance. Science, as we know it today, has its ascendance in the sixteenth and seventeenth centuries.

Galileo was in an esteemed group of people who like himself, could not live comfortably in the status quo. That group included Nicolaus Copernicus, Johannes Kepler, Christiaan Huygens, and Isaac Newton. Among twentieth and twenty-first century scientists, Galileo's name is above all others. Stephen Hawking stated that Galileo bears more responsibility for the emergence of modern science than anyone else and Albert Einstein called him the father of modern science.

It all started with Galileo's invention of the telescope in 1609. With this simple instrument, he had the ability to turn his eyes on the night sky and see things no one else saw. His observations were carefully formulated, and as time went on, most of his theories were proven correct.

How the world views science today, and how science views the world and the universe, well, you could say that was all Galileo's doing.

What we know about the universe today is nothing like what people believed in the Renaissance. Most people thought astronomy was completely ridiculous and relied on astrology to get them through their daily lives. Then there was the Catholic Church putting pressure on scientists to keep their opinions to themselves.

Galileo's legacy has been one of particular interest because of what happened to him in later life. Being tried and convicted by the Roman Inquisition was nothing to sneeze at. Being found guilty of heresy and condemned to house arrest was difficult for a man approaching his 70th birthday. Many views what happened to Galileo as one of the greatest tragedies and scandals of its day. According to Dr. Owen Gingerich, professor of astronomy at Harvard University, the Galileo controversy "essentially changed the way we do science because today science works primarily by persuasion and not by proof, and Galileo greatly influenced in making that happen."

Galileo could see through his telescope that what had been held as gospel truth by the Church for centuries was not true in the heavens above. When he tried to tell others about it, primarily in his book *Dialogue Concerning the Two Chief World Systems*, it was as if those two chief world systems collided head-on.

Suddenly everything educated people living in the Renaissance thought they knew about the Ptolemaic system was being shredded to bits by the Copernican system and Galileo's experiments. And it would take centuries for the world and the Catholic Church to come to its senses. Pope John Paul II began a highly publicized rehabilitation of Galileo from 1979-1992. In some ways, this only led to more controversy.

Which means that right into today, Galileo still fascinates. Whether you are a scientist, student, or someone with a penchant for learning, there is always something new to see regarding the relationship between religion and science, because it goes much further than just faith and reason. Galileo made it possible for the world to think for itself. There has always been governmental authority firmly established to keep people in their place, yet Galileo became a voice for individual freedom; something rarely seen or heard in the Renaissance era. He was one of many artists who opened up vistas for all to partake in. That led to more scientific research, and more political power, which in turn has resulted in revolutions and social and cultural change which is still transforming our world today.

You could say it all started with a basic telescope, which has led to grander innovations, such as the Hubble space telescope and the more recent Planck space observatory launched by the European Space Agency. Astronomers can now view the universe in greater detail and glory.

Today's telescopes have led to the discovery of more than 100 billion galaxies in the universe. As Pope Benedict XVI stated that "whoever looks at the cosmos following Galileo's lesson will not be able to stop only with that which he observes with a telescope; he will have to further proceed to ask himself about the meaning and end to which the whole of creation is oriented."

Galileo loved Scripture and often found great comfort in it. But he also believed that the Bible should not be taken literally or as an instrument for proving science. He was hoping that by this view, his detractors would be more inclined to work together to find those strands between faith and science which bind us all.

Galileo was an exceptional man. Living in an extraordinary time such as the Renaissance, it was only right that seeing things no one else was seeing; he had the forthrightness to speak the truth. No matter what people thought, or of what the consequences could be.

As Carl Sagan, creator of the Cosmos series, put it, "the nitrogen in our DNA, the calcium in our teeth, the iron in our blood, the carbon in our apple pies, were made in the interiors of collapsing stars. We are made of star stuff." Galileo Galilei would agree.

Conclusion

Despite his condemnation by the Catholic Church, Galileo has always remained a fascinating and famous person. He is considered a genius in scientific findings and particularly in his contributions to astronomy. In his day, astronomy was closely related to astrology, and many people had trouble telling the difference.

Galileo, however, knew better. He understood that the Earth moved and even when pressed to say otherwise, he still maintained his philosophy. He was aware that the Earth was not the center of the universe as the Church had been advocating for centuries, and he continued to stand up for this belief even in the face of imprisonment or death.

Galileo correctly identified the four moons of Jupiter: Io, Ganymede, Europa, and Callisto. In the 1990s when NASA sent a space mission to Jupiter, it was called Galileo in honor of the man who had been so closely entwined with it.

The world in which Galileo lived was just beginning to learn how to break free. Up until this time, people were always under the yoke of someone or something else. Peasants were beholden to their masters, people to the Church, women had to obey men and so on. Galileo was one of those few individuals who appear in every generation, who are unafraid to stand up to the biggest authorities and will not back down.

It was his telescope, after all, that put him in mind of things far beyond what was observed on Earth. Even the Catholic Church had to finally admit that the theories they had held onto were wrong.

It all started by looking at the sky and seeing beyond the borders; believing in what was there. Despite all of the protests and condemnations heaped upon him in his lifetime, Galileo was exonerated. He still stands tall today.